This book belongs to

....

For Sez—A.C.
For Evelyn—S.E.

Published in 2021 by Welbeck Editions
An Imprint of Welbeck Children's Limited, part of Welbeck Publishing Group.
20 Mortimer Street London W1T 3JW

Designer: Deborah Vickers
Designer: Kathryn Davies
Associate Publisher: Laura Knowles
Editor: Jenni Lazell

978-1-91351-946-9

Printed in Heshan, China

10 9 8 7 6 5 4 3 2 1

FSC
www.fsc.org
MIX
Paper from
responsible sources
FSC® C020056

All Things Change

WRITTEN BY

Anna Claybourne

ILLUSTRATED BY

Sarah Edmonds

WELBECK
EDITIONS

Contents

Everything changes

All the time, all around us, things are constantly changing. Day becomes night, then day again. The Moon sails across the sky, looking slightly different every night. Tides ebb and flow, plants sprout and grow, and birds hatch from their eggs to see the world for the first time. The seasons change and each brings a different kind of weather. This helps us decide what we do and where we go as the days and months pass by.

Our world, Earth, is part of a spinning, circling wheel of planets, constantly orbiting around a burning Sun. And we are changing too—growing older every day, learning new things, having new ideas, and changing our minds, sometimes within a split second.

Even things that seem to stand still are changing: the stars, the rocks, and the continents are all moving, shifting, and transforming, although we can't always see it. For anything to happen, something must change. In fact, without change, we wouldn't be here at all! This book explores the many kinds of change, and what they mean.

The Big Bang

Can you imagine a bigger change than *nothing* suddenly turning into *everything*? That's how we think the universe began. All the matter (or stuff) in the universe suddenly expanded from a single point, releasing vast amounts of energy in a burst known as the Big Bang.

What is the universe?

The universe includes everything we know of that exists, or has ever existed: the whole of space, all the planets, stars and moons, and Earth and everything on it—including plants, animals, and us humans. It's hard to imagine, but the Big Bang was the start of time, space, and everything in the universe. There wasn't anything before it.

From then to now

After the Big Bang, everything in the Universe kept spreading out, cooling, and changing. After about 370,000 years, atoms of matter began to form. This matter clumped together to make the first stars, and those stars clustered together to form huge galaxies, like our galaxy, the Milky Way. After nine billion years, our own star, the Sun, began to form.

Today, the universe is still expanding. Everything in it is moving farther apart, faster and faster. Old stars die, and new stars form.

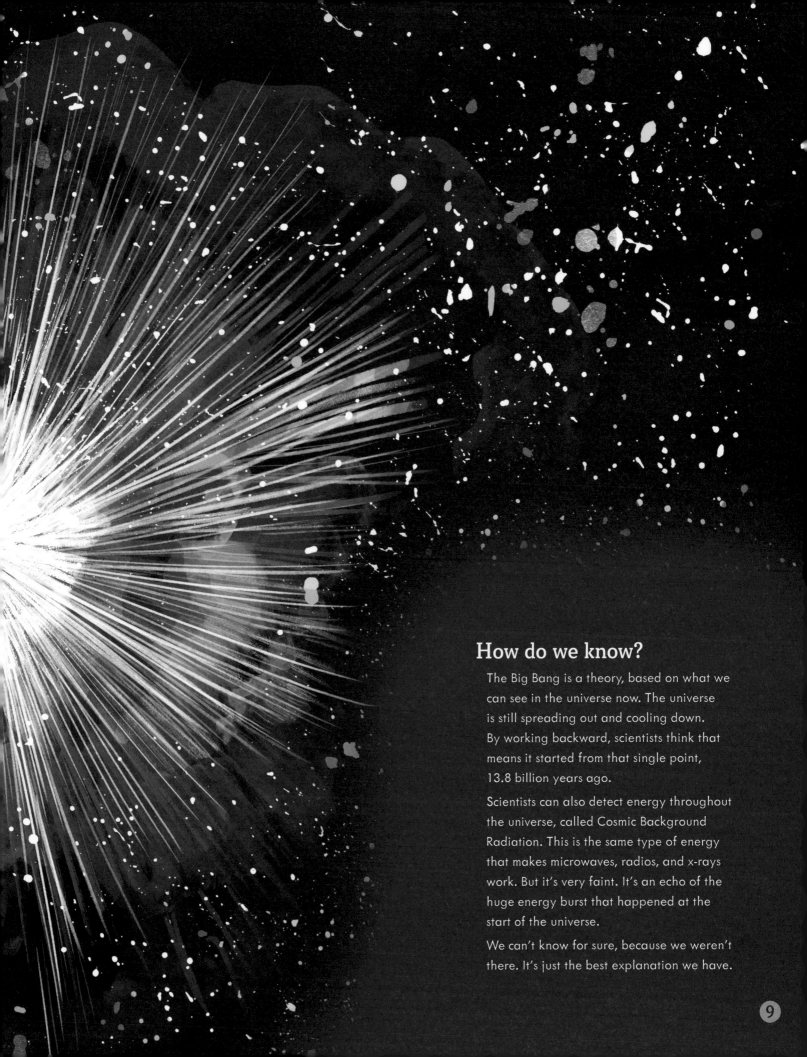

How do we know?

The Big Bang is a theory, based on what we can see in the universe now. The universe is still spreading out and cooling down. By working backward, scientists think that means it started from that single point, 13.8 billion years ago.

Scientists can also detect energy throughout the universe, called Cosmic Background Radiation. This is the same type of energy that makes microwaves, radios, and x-rays work. But it's very faint. It's an echo of the huge energy burst that happened at the start of the universe.

We can't know for sure, because we weren't there. It's just the best explanation we have.

The whirling planets

As you read this, you are sitting on a planet that's flying through space, orbiting the Sun at 66,500 miles per hour. That's about 18.6 miles every single second. At the same time, Earth spins around completely once every 24 hours. So, you are constantly looping the loop as you whirl around the Sun, faster than the fastest rocket.

Why can't you feel it?

You don't feel as if you're moving because you and this planet are all moving together. Since you're moving at the same speed you feel as if you're sitting still—just like when you're on a high-speed train or plane. You'd only notice Earth's movement if it were to suddenly slow down or speed up.

Asteroids

Jupiter

Saturn

Neptune

Uranus

The solar system

Earth is just one of eight planets, and many moons, asteroids, and comets, which orbit the Sun. Together, they make up the solar system. The solar system is in a constant state of change and motion. In fact, it can only exist that way. In the center, the Sun itself is spinning, and its powerful gravity pulls the planets towards it. At the same time, the planets' high-speed motion pulls them away. These forces balance each other out, so the planets keep moving on their path around the Sun.

The life of the Sun

Stars like our Sun have a lifetime of about 10 billion years. The Sun is almost halfway through its life. It will remain a ball of fiery gas, for another four or five billion years. Then it will expand, to become a red giant star before collapsing under its own gravity to form a much smaller white dwarf star. It will slowly cool down and stop burning. The dust and gas leftover from our Sun could eventually form new stars and planets.

Sun

Venus

Mercury

Moon

Earth

Mars

Where did the solar system come from?

The Sun is a star. It formed about 4.5 billion years ago, when hot gases and dust clumped together to form a spinning, glowing cloud. Over millions and million of years this cloud spread out into a disk. As the dust and gases within the disk bumped together, they formed all the objects we see in our solar system.

The changing Sun

10 billion years

nebula

yellow dwarf
(our Sun today)

red giant

white dwarf

The Seasons

As autumn arrives, the leaves turn from green to yellow, red and orange. It's a sign of the seasons changing, and another year going by. The seasons give the year a pattern, and shape our celebrations, holidays, and activities.

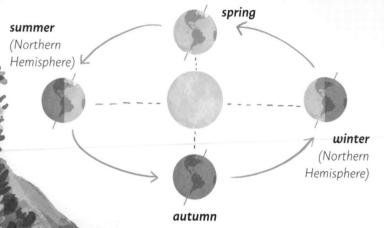

spring

summer
(Northern Hemisphere)

winter
(Northern Hemisphere)

autumn

What makes the seasons?

Seasons happen because Earth tilts as it orbits the Sun. Its northern and southern halves, or hemispheres, take turns leaning towards the Sun, then away from it. When the Northern Hemisphere leans away from the Sun, it has winter, while the Southern Hemisphere has summer. The equator gets a similar amount of sunshine all year round. The farther north or south you are, the more noticeable the seasons are.

Seasonal shifts

The world can look very different during just one year. The weather changes from warmer to colder, and back again. The daylight changes too, giving us longer, lighter days in summer, and short, dark days in winter.

Around you, nature changes with the seasons. In spring, trees grow new leaves, then flowers, then fruit in autumn. In winter, their branches are bare. Animals lay eggs and have babies in spring, so that the warmer weather gives them the best chance of survival. During the cold winter months, animals hide away, hibernate, or shelter in their dens and burrows, while snow blankets the ground.

Seasons long ago

Thousands of years ago, people had to survive the long, cold winter without much food, longing for spring to return. They learned to read the patterns of the seasons, so they knew when they would change. Some ancient peoples built circles of stone or earth to use as giant calendars. These used the position of the Sun to help them monitor the length of the days. They were designed so that on the shortest, darkest day of winter, the rising Sun would shine through a gateway or passageway. From that day on, they knew spring was on its way.

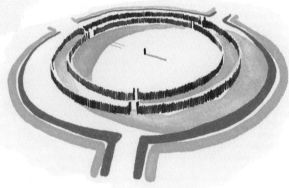

Sunrise on the shortest day at the Goseck circle, Germany, 4900 BCE

13

From day to night

In the daytime, the Sun floods the sky with light. Even if it's hidden by clouds, it lights up the world. But as the sun sinks below the horizon, the sky darkens and is lit by the glow of city lights and the twinkling of stars. While many creatures settle themselves to sleep, others are ready to venture out into the night.

day

night

In and out of the light

The spinning of Earth makes day and night happen. As the world turns on its axis, each part of it moves towards the Sun and into the light, then away from it into darkness. As your part of Earth moves into the light, the Sun seems to rise on the horizon. As you move away, you see the Sun sink, or set.

Nocturnal creatures

Nocturnal animals sleep in the day and come out at night. They have usually evolved to see well in the dark or use their ears and noses to find their way and hunt. Bats fly through the night to hunt moths and mosquitoes in the dark, while other creatures feel safe to venture out from underground homes into the cool darkness to forage for food.

Foxes prowl the cities and farms, raiding bins or chicken coops.

Daily rhythm

Humans are mostly diurnal, which means active during the day. In the morning, we get up, go to school or work, and do active things. When night comes, it's time to rest and recharge. The quiet darkness makes you feel sleepy. As you lie down and close your eyes, your brain starts to ignore sounds and sensations and you slip into an unconscious state. While your body rests, your brain sorts through your memories, deciding what to store and what to delete. And while this happens, you start to dream . . .

Crows settle in a flock to roost in trees.

Some plants close their leaves or petals for the night, while others have flowers that wait for night to fall to release their scent.

Ducks sleep on the water or bank, their heads folded on their backs.

The changing moon

The Moon appears to float across the sky and each time we
see it, it seems to be a slightly different shape. It grows from
a skinny crescent to a round, glowing orb, then shrinks back
down. At last it disappears, then starts again. These stages are
called the phases of the Moon.

Why does the Moon change?

The Moon doesn't really get bigger and smaller, or change
its shape. It's just the way we see it that changes. As it moves
around Earth, we see different amounts of it lit by the Sun.
The Moon appears to shine, but really it just reflects the
Sun's light. When it's behind Earth and opposite the Sun, we
see it fully lit up against the night sky—a full Moon.

The phases of the Moon

half Moon

waxing gibbous

waxing crescent

full Moon

new Moon

waning gibbous

waning crescent

half Moon

Moonlit nights

The full Moon is a beautiful, mesmerizing sight. Before we had street lights, moonlight lit up the land, allowing people to see their way at night. On a clear night, you can see the Moon's craters and "seas," or flat areas. They give it a mottled, patterned look, that over thousands of years people have tried to find meaning in, seeing in its surface faces and animals, or symbols of gods and goddesses. Religious festivals often take their dates from full Moons—like China's Mooncake Festival, held on the night of a full Moon in mid-autumn to celebrate the harvest.

Moon effects

The shining Moon in our skies has a great impact on our world. It influences the movement of the seas—the full Moon even triggers corals in the shallow seas to release their eggs into the water all at once, like an underwater snowstorm. Migrating birds can navigate by the Moon's light, while wildebeests are braver when the Moon is full, and wander farther to graze, able to see if hungry lions approach.

Nothing is absolute. Everything changes, everything moves, everything revolves, everything flies and goes away.

— FRIDA KAHLO, ARTIST

There is nothing permanent, except change.

— HERACLITUS, **PHILOSOPHER**

Nothing happens until something moves.

— ALBERT EINSTEIN, **SCIENTIST**

Making mountains

Rock might seem as if it lasts forever, but it doesn't. Like everything else, rocks change over time—a very, very long time—but mountains will still be here long after we are gone.

Jigsaw Earth

Earth's crust is made up of huge sections, or plates. They sit on top of hot, partly melted rock inside Earth, fitting together like puzzle pieces. They're slowly moving, too—about as fast as your fingernails grow.

Folds and faults

In some places, Earth's plates push together. The rock they are made of gets squeezed and crumpled, and folded upward. This is how mountain ranges such as the Himalayas, which are over 50 million years old, are formed. In other places, cracks—or faults—in Earth's surface open up, forcing large blocks of rock up and down.

Wearing away

Rock is constantly wearing away, especially on high, cold, windy mountainsides. Water seeps into cracks, freezes, and splits rocks apart. Wind and rain gradually batter and break rocks down. This process of change is called erosion. Gravity pulls rock fragments downhill, where they fall into rivers, and are washed away to the sea, collecting on the seabed in layers of sand, mud, and pebbles. Gradually, these fragments get squashed down, and harden into sedimentary rock.

Making diamonds

Where plates crush together, the heat and pressure can change some rocks into a different type of material. Graphite—which is used to make pencil leads—can be transformed deep within the earth into hard, clear, glittering diamonds.

Rock recycling

Like recycled bottles or tin cans, old rocks can get broken down or melt so they form new rocks inside the Earth. It just takes a very, very long time. Any rock or pebble you find and pick up could have been recycled over and over by our planet.

An island is born

We have discovered every land on this planet . . .
so far! Sometimes the world can surprise us with
a brand new island, created by the eruption of
an undersea volcano.

New land

On November 14, 1963, a cook on a fishing boat to the south
of Iceland spotted a column of smoke rising from the water.
Thinking a small boat must be on fire, the fishing boat went to
help. Instead, the crew found the water bubbling and boiling,
with smoke and ash pouring from the sea surface, and red-hot
glowing rocks shooting into the air. Under the sea, a volcano
was erupting, forming a mound of cooled lava and ash.

The eruption continued for almost four years, finally
stopping when the new island, named Surtsey, was about
a mile across, with a peak 570 feet high—as tall as a
skyscraper. Gradually, grass and other plants have grown
on it, and animals have moved in too. No humans live there,
but scientists visit to study it.

Out of a volcano

All land changes slowly over time, but volcanic forces can make it change much, much faster. When a volcano erupts, hot molten rock, or lava, flows out. It comes from inside Earth, where the temperature is much hotter than on the surface. When it meets the air or water, the lava cools and hardens, forming new volcanic rocks.

As well as forming new land, volcanic eruptions can be incredibly destructive. In 1883, Krakatoa, an island volcano in Indonesia, blew itself up in an enormous, explosive eruption. Two thirds of the island was destroyed, and became ocean.

layers of lava and ash

magma vent

side vent

magma chamber

The water cycle

Have you ever wondered where rain comes from? All the water on our planet is constantly changing and moving around and around in an endlessly repeating cycle.

Moving water

Water flows downhill from mountains in small streams, joining together into rivers, which flow into lakes and oceans. Some of the water evaporates into the air, becoming fog, dew, or clouds. It falls from the sky as rain and snow, soaks into the ground, and gets absorbed by plants and trees, helping them to grow.

Water vapour rises into the sky. As it gets higher and colder, it condenses into water droplets, which form clouds.

Water evaporates from rivers and seas in the Sun's heat, and escapes from the leaves of plants.

Wind blows clouds back over the land. As clouds rise higher, they get colder, and the water droplets get bigger.

The same water

Through the water cycle, the same water gets recycled over and over again. When you fill a glass with water from the tap, that water has probably been around for billions of years. Water molecules in your glass will have passed through dinosaurs, plants, and other people before you, as well as through rivers, lakes, clouds, and oceans.

The water falls as rain, snow, or hail. It flows into streams, which flow into rivers, which flow down to the sea.

Some water soaks into underground rocks— this is called groundwater.

Water of life

All living things need water, not just humans. Plants suck it up through their roots, using it to grow and build more plant parts. In animals, it flows between and through body cells and makes up most of our blood.

Turning to stone

How does a living thing change into a stone fossil? It happens slowly, often taking hundreds or thousands of years, and leaving behind just a trace of what once was ...

A story of change

Fossils show us how life has changed over time. They reveal creatures that lived long ago, but are now extinct. Ammonites were prehistoric sea creatures, similar to octopuses, but with a ridged, snail-like shell. When an ammonite died it sank onto the seabed. Its soft body rotted away or was eaten, leaving just the shell behind.

Gradually, layers of mud or sand collected on top, and were squashed down until they turned into stone. Water containing dissolved rocks and minerals soaked through the stone into the shell, and the minerals began to collect in the tiny gaps. Sometimes, all of the real shell dissolved away, leaving just the rocks or minerals in the same shape, like a cast.

HOW AN AMMONITE BECAME A FOSSIL

ammonite dies

shell is buried in the seabed

Trapped in time

Some fossils were formed when insects became trapped in sticky tree resin, which hardened into amber. They are so perfectly preserved, you could imagine that they could come flying out, even though they have been encased in amber for millions of years.

pterosaur

Fossil myths

Since prehistoric times, people have found fossils in the ground, and wondered what they were. They looked like plants and animals, but they were made of stone. All over the world, there are ancient tales of dragons and giants, perhaps inspired by the fossilized bones and skeletons of huge dinosaurs and pterosaurs.

shell is replaced with minerals

Rusting away

This forgotten shipwreck has spilled its cargo of treasures across the seabed. Some human-made things still glint and shine, but others have been marked by the passage of time and covered in a layer of corroding rust.

Oxidization

During the many centuries this treasure lay at the bottom of the sea, the salt and oxygen in the seawater reacted with anything containing iron, coating it with a thick, reddish oxide, or rust. Continual oxidization leads to the rust peeling off the metal and weakening it.

Other metals oxidize in different ways. Copper and bronze, for example, change color over time to gain a pretty blue-ish green layer known as a patina. You can see it on bronze sculptures and on some buildings and roofs.

A sea change

When steel ships sink, they also oxidize, growing a coating of reddish iron rust. Barnacles, corals, and limpets grow all over sunken ships, encrusting them with a colorful living layer. Fish and other sea creatures make their homes within the wreck, while divers explore their dark depths.

Unchanging gold

Some metals react easily with their surroundings, and turn to rust. But gold is very stable. It hardly ever reacts with anything, and therefore keeps its value. So, after centuries at the bottom of the sea, a hoard of gold coins will be almost as good as new.

Carving the land

The water in this river is fluid and soft. It doesn't feel like something that could cut through rock. But, over time, waves and rivers have the ability to drastically carve and shape the land it touches.

Carving valleys

As a river flows along toward the sea, it washes away soil and rock. In some places, if the ground is soft or dissolves easily, the river will keep cutting deeper into the land. As more and more rock dissolves or crumbles, the river carries it along, tumbling the rocks until they are smooth and round, and washing them toward the sea. Over thousands or millions of years, a river can carve a huge valley, or a deep canyon or gorge. You can often see layers of different rocks in its sides or walls.

Crashing on the cliffs

The tide rises and falls, and waves roll in from the sea and constantly batter the coast. Waves can make cliffs crumble and collapse, bit by bit, or eat away from underneath to hollow out sea caves. In some places, waves slowly eat away at the shore, and houses that were built far inland find themselves on the edge of a cliff, then fall into the sea.

Dripping water

In limestone caves, water soaks through the rock, dissolving minerals as it goes. It drips from the ceiling, leaving behind a tiny bit of limestone where it falls. Where it lands, it leaves more stone. Over time, the dripping water builds hanging fingers of stone, or stalactites, and skinny stone towers on the ground, called stalagmites.

Stalactites hold on tight.

Stalagmites grow with all their might.

Hag stones

Some pebbles are made of both hard and soft rock. When water wears away at the soft rock, it can make a hole all the way through the stone. Called hag stones or adder stones, these pebbles with natural, slowly formed holes in them are said to have magical powers.

31

Freezing over

For most of the year, this lake was full of flowing water. If you threw a pebble in, it made ripples. But now, everything has changed. The water has become solid, slippery, rock-hard ice, so thick you can walk on it.

Freeze and thaw

Water changes from liquid to solid depending on its temperature. When it gets cold enough, reaching 32°F (0°C) or below, its molecules lock together in a lattice, and it freezes into solid ice. As the temperature rises, the water on the surface of the ice liquifies. It thaws and drips, or melts into puddles.

The world's ice

The world is coldest at the north and south poles, and at the tops of the highest mountains. Most of the water there is frozen into ice. As snow falls, it collects, packs down into solid ice, and slowly flows downhill as a glacier—a river of ice. Where a glacier meets the sea, chunks break off and become icebergs that drift the world's oceans.

Everything changes

These changes between solid, liquid, and gas are called changes of state. Other things change their state too—it happens all around us. We melt glass, metals, and plastic to mold them into useful shapes, which then cool into solid objects. A camping stove burns gas, but it's stored in the canister as a liquid. You can melt butter in a pan, and melt chocolate in your mouth.

Ice crystals

Snowflakes form when water vapour freezes around a speck of dust or pollen particle high in the atmosphere. The water molecules then arrange themselves in a six-sided structure around the tiny speck and the snowflake grows as it falls to the ground. Because of the conditions in which it was formed, each snowflake is totally unique.

The Tide

In just a few hours, this beach will become the seabed. Slowly, bit by bit, the sea will rise higher and higher, creeping up the seashore and covering the sand. Then, just as gradually, it will flow back, leaving the beach rinsed clean.

Ebb and flow

Around the world the tide happens twice a day, every day. Seawater ebbs and flows, going out and in, out and in, as if the sea is breathing. As the tide flows in over a sandy beach, it smooths the sand, washing away your sandcastles, footprints, and drawings. When it ebbs away, it leaves behind small seashells, pebbles, sea glass, and driftwood, carried ashore by the waves.

Rock pools

The high tide fills hollows in the shoreline rocks with seawater, and when the tide goes out, rock pools are left behind. These pools are a safe home for sea creatures. Look closely, and you might see . . .

tiny fish

sea worms

crab

What makes the tides?

Tides happen because of the Moon. The Moon, like Earth, has its own gravity, or pulling force. It pulls on the sea, making it bulge upward. Earth constantly spins around, giving us day and night. As your part of the world moves past the Moon, the bulge of water creates a high tide.

Low tide

High tide

Moon

High tide

Low tide

Seashore life

The ever-changing seashore between high and low tide is full of life. When the tide goes out, clams and lugworms burrow under the sand to stay safe and damp. Seabirds use their long beaks to dig down and find them. Limpets clamp their shells onto rocks and hide inside.

When the tide comes in, bladder wrack seaweed floats to the surface of the sea using its gas-filled "bladders" to catch the sunshine. Barnacles open their shells, reaching out with their tentacles to find food. Sea snails emerge from their shells, and sea stars crawl across the seabed.

small octopus

sea anemone

sea star

35

The changing sky

Whenever you go outside, you're surrounded by the huge, endless sky. It's like a giant arena showing a constantly changing performance of light and color, sunshine and clouds, storms and rain. In just one day, the sky can transform itself many times over, from countless shades of blue, to ominous dark storm clouds.

Approaching storms

The day could start with a clear blue sky, promising a hot, sunny summer's day. But, far away, clouds are gathering on the horizon, piling up into a fluffy tower with a dark, menacing base. As winds blow the clouds closer, you feel a chilly breeze. Suddenly, a downpour begins. There's a warm, earthy smell as the hot, dusty ground gets soaked. BOOM! Lightning flashes light up the gloomy sky, and its thundering sound reaches you seconds later.

At last, the storm dies down. The last few clouds blow away, dropping their last raindrops. The Sun is revealed again. Shining on the retreating rain, the light is split into a beautiful rainbow.

The atmosphere scatters the Sun's light, making the whole sky look blue.

Why does the weather change?

The sky we see above and around us is the atmosphere, which is the layer of air around Earth. The air in the atmosphere is constantly heating up in the sunshine, in different places as the days, nights and seasons change. The warmer air rises and spreads out, meeting currents of cooler air as it swirls around our planet. The atmosphere also contains water vapour, and as air cools, this water forms clouds, then rain, snow, or hail. Thunderstorms happen when ice and raindrops inside clouds rub together, building up an electric charge.

Tales of the rainbow

As the Sun shines through raindrops, they split its light into a spectrum of colors, making a rainbow. In Norse mythology, the rainbow is a bridge linking Earth to Asgard, the home of the gods. In Australian Aboriginal legends, it's the Rainbow Serpent, who created Earth, arching through the sky as it moves from one waterhole to another.

Burning up

In hot, dry weather, trees and grass dry out, and are easily set alight. The flames spread fast, leading to a raging forest fire that threaten everything in its path.

Destructive sparks

A spark from a careless campfire or a dropped match could start a forest fire. But they can also start naturally, ignited by a lightning strike, or just by the Sun's intense heat. As a wildfire takes hold, it spreads into the treetops, and burns hotter and hotter. Sparks blow on the wind, carrying the fire across roads and rivers. Animals flee from the heat, burrowing into the ground, flying into the air, or just running for their lives. After the fire has passed by, it leaves a blackened, scorched landscape behind.

Cleansing fire

A forest fire is also part of a natural cycle of change. Wildfires have always happened, and even though they burn trees down, they also keep forests healthy and strong. The fire clears old, dead wood and fallen leaves. It turns them into ash, full of useful chemicals that feed the soil and make it more fertile. It kills harmful tree diseases, and makes space to let the sunlight in, so that new, young trees can sprout. Unfortunately, climate change is causing bigger and more frequent forest fires, leaving wildlife with smaller and smaller spaces to live in.

What happens when things burn?

When something burns, it changes. In fact, it mostly disappears. When a fuel like wood burns, chemicals in the fuel break apart, and react with oxygen in the air. This creates new chemicals, mainly water vapour and carbon dioxide gas. These gases are invisible, and escape into the air. The burning process releases energy, in the form of light and heat. Afterwards, |all that remains is a grayish, dusty ash.

Fiery birth

Some trees are fire-resistant: even though they seem burned, they soon bud and grow again when the fire has gone. The Jack pine tree of North America has special cones, called serotinous cones. They are tightly sealed until the heat of a forest fire opens them, releasing their seeds.

The changing climate

For the past 200 years, Earth's climate has been warming up due to human activities. In turn, this creates more change for us all.

Natural changes

Climate means the weather pattern in a particular place, whether that's a small town, or the whole planet. Over time, climate can change. We know that Earth's climate has been through much hotter times and much colder times, known as ice ages.

From warmer ...

55 million years ago, the average temperature on Earth was about 73°F (23°C), 13°F (7°C) warmer than today. There was no ice, and the sea level was up to 197 feet higher than it is today. Antarctica was warm and full of plants and animals.

...to colder

The coldest part of the last ice age was 20,000 years ago, with average temperatures of about 43°F (6°C), 17°F (10°C) colder than today. Vast amounts of water froze into ice around the north and south poles, in glaciers and on cold mountaintops. At this time, the continent of North America was still connected to northern Asia.

Global warming

Today, the world is warming up again, but the way humans live means this process is happening much faster. Our engines, machines, and power stations burn huge amounts of fuel, adding carbon dioxide to the air. As our farm animals digest food, they add methane gas to the air. These are greenhouse gases. They trap the Sun's heat in the atmosphere, making the planet warmer.

The changes ahead

The increasing temperature is causing other changes too, such as rising sea levels, extreme weather, and hotter, drier areas where crops cannot grow. Changing habitats also make it hard for wildlife to survive, so we all need to do our part to make global warming slow down.

When you get into
a tight place,
and everything
goes against you...
never give up then,
for that is just the time
and place that the tide
will turn.

— HARRIET BEECHER STOWE, **AUTHOR**

We cannot direct the wind, but we can adjust the sails.

— DOLLY PARTON, **SINGER AND SONGWRITER**

Everything changes, even Stone.

— CLAUDE MONET, **ARTIST**

Life cycles

Being alive means being in a constant cycle of change. All living things grow, change, and give way to the next generation, over and over again.

Endless cycles

Each plant, animal, or other creature begins its life, then grows to become an adult. Then it may reproduce, or have babies, to make more living things like itself. Finally, it grows old and dies—and its young repeat the cycle. This is how species, or types, of living things keep existing. Any living thing you can think of, from bacteria or mushrooms to a snow leopard, a rose bush or you yourself, is at a particular point in its life cycle.

Transformation

Humans and other mammals start off small and grow bigger, but look similar throughout their lives. Some creatures, however, change completely. This kind of change is called metamorphosis.

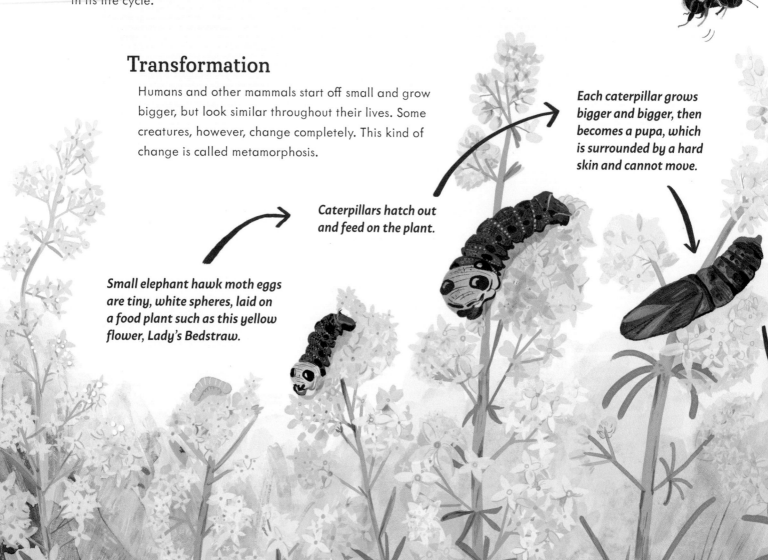

Each caterpillar grows bigger and bigger, then becomes a pupa, which is surrounded by a hard skin and cannot move.

Caterpillars hatch out and feed on the plant.

Small elephant hawk moth eggs are tiny, white spheres, laid on a food plant such as this yellow flower, Lady's Bedstraw.

Cycles of life

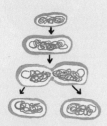

Bacteria reproduce by growing, then dividing in two.

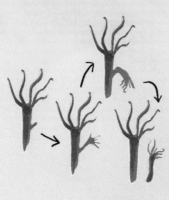

A hydra is a tiny sea creature that has babies by budding. A baby hydra buds or grows from a larger one, then breaks off.

Frog eggs hatch into tadpoles, which gradually lose their tails and grow into adult frogs.

Birds lay eggs, and the chick grows inside, before hatching out and growing bigger into adult birds.

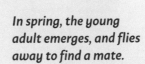

In spring, the young adult emerges, and flies away to find a mate.

After a male and female mate, the female lays her eggs on a Lady's Bedstraw plant.

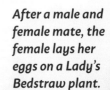

Inside, the caterpillar does not simply grow wings and other moth parts. Instead, its body breaks down completely, turning into a kind of slime. All its body chemicals are rearranged, building the new, adult moth.

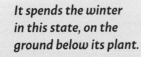

It spends the winter in this state, on the ground below its plant.

The Secrets of seeds

A tiny seed can change and grow into something as big,
tall and strong as an oak tree. But takes a lot of sunlight,
air, water, and time—and plenty of luck.

The time is right ...

A seed such as an acorn can wait a long time until it has what it
needs to start growing. When it's warm and sunny enough, and
the ground is damp, the acorn sprouts, growing one root down
into the soil, and another shoot up into the air. It uses the sun's
energy to grow bigger, using water from the soil and carbon
dioxide gas from the air.

By about five years old, it's a young tree, or sapling. At 30 or 40
years of age, it's an adult oak tree. Then, the tree grows fluffy,
dangling catkins, and tiny, bud-shaped flowers that can turn
into more acorns, which will make more new oak trees. Over
hundreds of years, millions of acorns grow and fall.

Ancient oak

600 or 700 years later, the oak is an old tree. It makes fewer acorns, but its trunk still grows wider every year. An ancient oak's trunk can be as wide as a house. As an oak tree grows, it becomes a home for birds, insects, and other animals. Ants make nests among the roots, beetles burrow under the bark, and robins and jays nest in the branches.

Tree rings

Every spring, a tree grows a new layer of wood around its trunk. The growth slows down in autumn, forming harder, darker wood. One light ring and one dark ring equals one year of growth, showing us a record of the changing seasons. This is how tree rings are made.

47

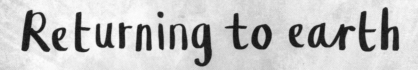

Returning to earth

When a living thing dies, its body returns to the earth where it becomes part of a bigger cycle of life. Growth and decay are two sides of the same coin on this forest floor, where the death of one creature can contribute to the life of another.

Cycle of life

When bodies decompose, they break down into their basic ingredients. These ingredients become useful nutrients in the soil, making it richer and more fertile. Plants soak up the nutrients, which helps them to grow. The same plants become food for animals that are then eaten by other animals. These nutrients move around and around, passing through many different living things over time.

Hyenas, crows, and vultures are scavengers that feed on dead animals, or carrion. Scavenging helps to break down dead bodies, and scavengers poop out some nutrients, too.

Decomposers

Living things called decomposers feed on dead plants and animals, helping to break them down. If it wasn't for them, dead plant and animal matter would pile up on Earth's surface.

Rotting

If you leave food lying around for long enough, fungi or bacteria find it and start to grow, making the food rot away and smell bad. This is no good for you, but if you put your leftover fruit and vegetables in a compost heap, earthworms and millipedes can turn it into rich compost that plants love to grow in.

Bacteria grow on dead plants and animals. They release chemicals that break down and dissolve their food, so they can soak up the chemicals they need. The rest crumbles away.

Fungi include mushrooms and mold. They grow on dead, rotting plants, logs, and animals, and reach into them with their tiny thread-like roots, making them slowly disintegrate into soil.

Earthworms and millipedes feed on dead leaves and decaying matter in the soil. It passes through their bodies and comes out as poop that improves the soil.

49

Evolution

We know from fossils that long ago, life on Earth was very different than how it is now. That's because ever since life began, it has been changing over billions of years, in a process called evolution.

How did life start?

All living things on Earth today evolved from one early single cell, known as LUCA, or the Last Universal Common Ancestor. This first living thing must have appeared around four billion years ago. No one knows exactly where it came from, but it could have formed in a deep undersea vent full of minerals, or a bubbling mud pool.

How life evolves

Living things are made up of cells that contain genes, which are strings of information that control how the living thing grows and works. All living things can also reproduce, or copy themselves. When they do this, they copy their genes into new cells. During this process, slight changes can happen.

Often this makes no difference, but sometimes it changes something about the living thing—its size, color, or shape, for example. If a change makes it easier for a living thing to survive, it will live longer and pass on this useful change to its offspring. This can lead to a new type of living thing, that eventually becomes a new, separate species. Over billions of years, this has happened many times. That's how one living thing evolved into all the incredible and varied life forms that exist today.

Some creatures were once bigger than they are today. The giant Meganeura dragonfly lived around 300 million years ago and had a wingspan of over 27.5 in.

tetrapod

A human timeline

Like everything alive today, humans evolved through millions of tiny changes. Our species has only been here for 300,000 years—a tiny amount of time compared to the dinosaurs, for example.

early humans

2.5 m.y.a

the first multi-celled creatures

2,100 m.y.a

four-legged tetrapods that moved onto the land

395 m.y.a

reptiles

340 m.y.a

large, monkey-like mammals

79.6 m.y.a

apes that walked upright on the ground

20 m.y.a

the first animals

610 m.y.a

fish

505 m.y.a

the first mammals (small, rat-like creatures)

220 m.y.a

tree-dwelling apes

63 m.y.a

(m.y.a = million years ago)

Dinosaurs lived from 243 million years ago until 66 million years ago. Look at how this dinosaur evolved into a bird.

theropod dinosaur

archaeopteryx (believed to be the first bird)

bird

The tree of life

Evolution has created a tree-like pattern, sometimes called the tree of life. More and more new species have branched off, like new branches, twigs, and leaves. While some die, others keep growing and lead to new branches.

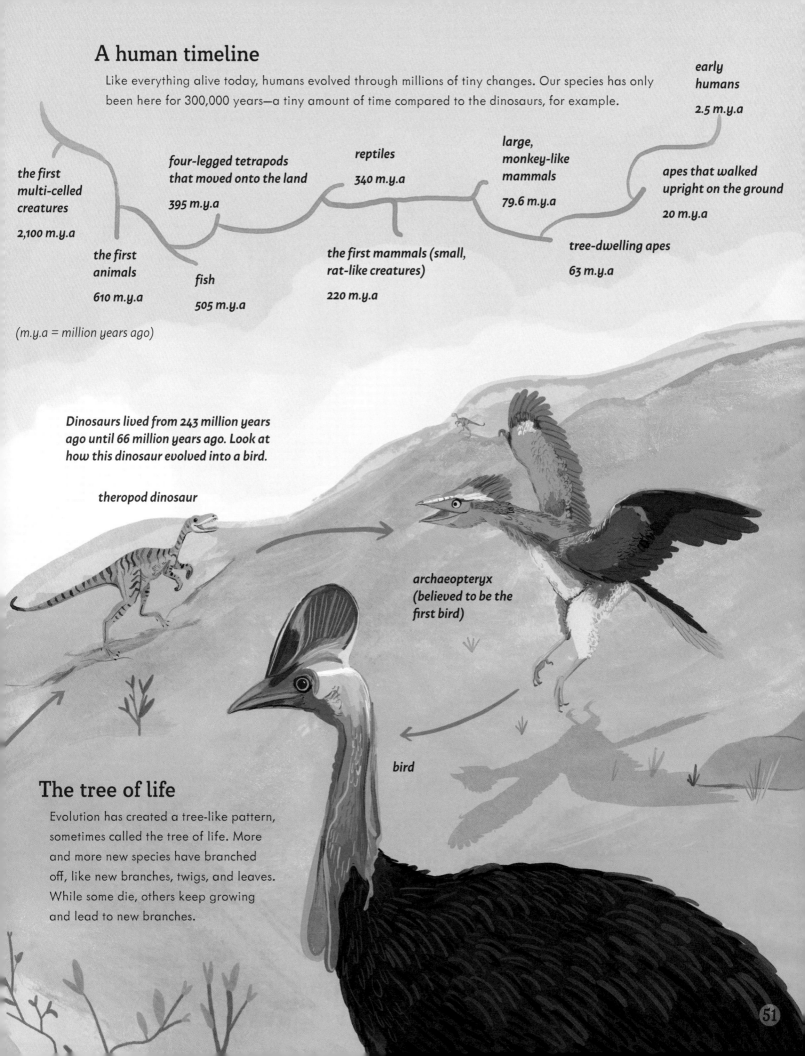

Change will not come if we wait for some other person or some other time. We are the ones we've been waiting for. We are the change that we seek.

— BARACK OBAMA,
FORMER PRESIDENT OF THE UNITED STATES

To bring about change,
you must not be afraid
to take the first step.

— ROSA PARKS, **CIVIL RIGHTS ACTIVIST**

And change is coming
whether you like it
or not.

— GRETA THUNBERG, **CLIMATE ACTIVIST**

From young to old

When humans are first born, we rely on others to keep us safe and well. It takes years of changing, learning, and growing to develop from a child into an adult. And we keep on changing after that, too.

Growing up

As children get older, their bones grow, making them taller. Most people reach their adult height between about 15 and 18. You develop more body cells to make more skin and muscle. Teenagers' bodies change too, as they become adults. But the human brain isn't completely grown up until we are about 25!

Tiny babies

Newborn babies need someone to look after them, feed them, and keep them warm. As they grow, babies look at, touch, and grab everything they can. They wriggle, roll, crawl, and finally learn to walk and talk. Everything they do, sense, and experience helps their brain grow, as they learn about the world.

Starting to shrink

Between 30 and 70 years of age, you'll probably become around one to two inches shorter—and shrink even more after that. This happens as leg bones wear down at the ends, and the bones in your back get more squashed together.

Old and wrinkly

Our bodies make chemicals that give our hair its color, and make our skin soft and elastic. As we get older, we stop making so much of them. That's why older people's hair becomes white, and their skin looks wrinkled. Wrinkles appear where you have moved your face the most. They are like a story of your life.

Changing brains

As we learn, new connections form between our brain cells. This happens fastest in babies, but it keeps happening throughout your life—as you learn new skills, like reading, swimming, drawing, or playing an instrument, and absorb information, like words, names, and numbers.

Children and young people are faster at learning, and better at remembering things. As you get older, your brain learns more slowly, but you have more stored knowledge and wisdom.

Living through changes

Do you ever feel like you are not the same person you were a year ago? It's not just our age and physical self that changes. We constantly experience change in our lives, and our thoughts, ideas, and feelings change, too. Sometimes it can even feel as if we change from one moment to the next.

Experiences change us

Throughout our lives, we learn, grow, and change because of the things that happen to us and around us. Good and bad experiences can influence our lives. Learning to swim, for example, can feel a bit scary at first. It takes time to get the hang of floating and moving your body in the right way so you don't sink. A bad experience might put you off for a while, but it's best to keep trying. Over time, you will gain more confidence in your abilities and can challenge yourself in new ways.

Changing your mind

People often change their minds about all kinds of things. This can be because they experience and learn more, or just because there can be different ways of seeing a situation. Hearing about other people's experiences and ideas can change what you think too, and so can discussing and debating different topics. Even scientists change their minds when they find new evidence. It's okay to change your mind!

Fleeting feelings

Moods and feelings change all the time —sometimes from day to day, or even from minute to minute. The smallest actions can change how you feel at any moment, such as someone smiling at you, cuddling a pet, or a cloud covering the Sun. If you think about it, it's only because things change that we feel anything at all. You only really know what happiness feels like, for example, because you don't feel it all the time.

Accepting change

As this book shows, change is normal. We're surrounded by large and small changes all the time, and we all go though many changes in our lives. Yet change can be hard. Some people find it really scary or stressful. Sometimes, you just don't want things to change!

Why is change hard?

Change can be difficult, even if you want it to happen. If you don't, it's even worse. You get used to things being the way they are—surroundings, friends, and everyday routines. If any of these things has to change, it can feel weird and uncomfortable. Especially if the change is out of your control, and you have to deal with moving to a new town, or a whole new country, or having to say goodbye to someone you love.

Coping with change

In everyone's life, change is going to happen, one way or another. Learning to accept it, and make the changes you want to, is very useful. Preparing and planning for a change helps you cope with it when it comes. Getting used to a change can take time, but bit by bit, it gets easier.

Changes can bring new, wonderful opportunities, and make life more interesting. They can lead to new discoveries and take you to places you never imagined! And, although change can be hard, it's much better than nothing ever changing at all.

How long does change take?

Some changes happen in the blink of an eye, and others take months, centuries, or millions of years. Compare them at a glance!

SOLAR SYSTEM'S ORBIT AROUND THE MILKY WAY GALAXY

230 MILLION YEARS

THE LIFETIME OF A **STAR**

10 BILLION YEARS

66 MILLION YEARS

TIME SINCE THE **DINOSAURS** DIED OUT

TIME IT TOOK THE **HIMALAYAS** TO FORM

10 MILLION YEARS

1,000 YEARS

TIME IT TOOK FOR WATER TO CARVE THE **GRAND CANYON**

6 MILLION YEARS

300,000 YEARS

LIFETIME OF AN **OAK TREE**

HOW LONG **MODERN HUMANS** HAVE EXISTED

EARTH'S **ORBIT** AROUND THE SUN

1 YEAR

5 WEEKS

LIFETIME OF AN ADULT
SMALL ELEPHANT HAWK MOTH

MOON'S ORBIT AROUND THE EARTH

27 DAYS

AVERAGE LIFETIME OF A **SNOW LEOPARD**

20 YEARS

ONE FULL ROTATION OF THE **EARTH**

24 HOURS

TIME IT TAKES THE **TIDE** TO COME IN AND GO OUT

24 HOURS AND 50 MINUTES

72 YEARS

AVERAGE LIFETIME OF A **HUMAN**

ONE HUMAN **EYE-BLINK**

1/10 OF A SECOND

Glossary

ASTEROIDS millions of small, rocky objects that orbit the Sun. Most of them are in the asteroid belt between the orbits of Mars and Jupiter.

ATMOSPHERE the layer of gases surrounding a planet or star.

ATOMS tiny particles that make up the basic building blocks of all matter in the Universe.

CARBON DIOXIDE a colorless and odorless gas that humans and animals breathe out, and that is formed by burning fuels, and the decomposition of animal and plant matter. Plants absorb carbon dioxide from the air in photosynthesis.

CELL the basic building block of plants and animals (and humans).

CLIMATE CHANGE any significant long-term change in the typical weather conditions of a region, or the whole Earth.

CLIMATE the typical weather conditions in a place.

COMET a big ball made up of frozen gases, rocks, dust, and ice that orbits the Sun.

CORRODING the gradual wearing away of the surface of materials (like metal) by a chemical reaction caused by their environment.

DECOMPOSITION the decay of organic matter (such as plants and animals).

DIURNAL being active or happening during the day rather than at night.

ECOSYSTEM a community of living things and the environment they live in.

ENDANGERED a species of plant or animal that is in danger of becoming extinct because of major threats to its habitat or because only a few of its type remain.

ENVIRONMENT the surroundings or living space of a living thing.

EROSION the process in which Earth's surface (rocks or soil) is worn away by the effects of weather, water, or ice.

EVOLUTION the process by which living things change and develop over time.

EVOLVE to undergo evolution, to change or develop gradually.

EXTINCT a species of plant or animal that has died out (is no longer in existence).

FOSSIL the preserved remains or traces of dead insects, animals, and plants that lived long ago. The process by which a fossil is formed is called fossilization.

GALAXY a huge collection of stars, solar systems, dust, and gas, all held together by gravity. The galaxy that our solar system is in is called the Milky Way.

GLOBAL WARMING an increase in the average temperature of Earth's atmosphere.

GRAVITY the force that makes objects pull toward the center of Earth.

GREENHOUSE EFFECT when the greenhouse gases in Earth's atmosphere build up too much and trap heat, making the Earth warmer. This leads to global warming.

GREENHOUSE GASES the gases (including carbon dioxide and methane) in Earth's atmosphere that stop the Sun's heat from escaping, instead trapping it in the atmosphere and warming the planet.

HABITAT the natural home or environment of a living thing.

HEMISPHERE half of a sphere. The Earth is divided into the Northern and Southern Hemispheres by the equator.

HIBERNATE the long period of deep sleep that some animals have during cold weather.

LAVA magma that flows onto Earth's surface from a volcano or crack in Earth's crust, and which then cools and hardens into rock.

MAGMA hot, melted or partly melted rock under Earth's surface.

METAMORPHOSIS the process which some animals go through to change into their adult form, for example, from a caterpillar to a butterfly.

MIGRATE the seasonal movement of animals from one place to another.

MOLTEN something that is melted or reduced to a liquid form by intense heat.

NEBULA a cloud of gas and dust in space.

ORBIT the continuous movement of an object around a star or planet.

ORGANISM a form of life (such as a plant, animal, fungus, or bacteria) that is made of one or more cells.

OXIDATION when a substance (such as rock) gains oxygen.

OXYGEN a colorless and odorless gas that is essential for plants and animals to live, and which makes up about 20% of Earth's atmosphere.

PHOTOSYNTHESIS the process by which plants make food from water and carbon dioxide.

PTEROSAUR flying reptiles that lived at the same time as the dinosaurs.

PUPA an insect that is in the stage of development between a larva and a fully grown adult. It is enclosed in a protective case called a cocoon.

RED GIANT a giant star that is near the end of its life, which has cooled and swollen in size.

RUST the flaky, brown material caused as a result of the chemical reaction of iron with water and oxygen.

SOLAR SYSTEM the Sun and the planets that move around it.

SPECIES a particular type of living thing.

TECTONIC PLATES the huge sections of rock that make up Earth's surface.

TETRAPODS four footed animals.

THEROPOD a carnivorous dinosaur that usually walked on two legs.

UNIVERSE the whole of space and everything that it contains.

WHITE DWARF the small, compacted remains of a dead star.

YELLOW DWARF a medium-sized star. Our Sun is a yellow dwarf star.

Index